The Slug Manual

The Rise and Fall of Criticism

Jennifer James, Ph.D.

BRONWEN PRESS / Seattle, Washington

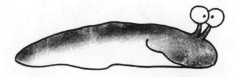

Requests for such permissions should be addressed to:
Bronwen Press
3903 East James
Seattle, Washington 98122

Printed in the United States of America

Library of Congress Cataloging in Publication Data

James, Jennifer, 1943-
    The Slug Manual

    1. Invective – Anecdotes, facetiae, satire, etc. 2. Interpersonal communication – Anecdotes, facetiae, satire, etc. I. Title.
PN6231.I65J36   1986   818'.5402   86-2303

ISBN 0-915423-01-4

ACKNOWLEDGEMENTS

This book was conceived in the Northwest where slugs abound. One day on my radio program in Seattle I was discussing criticism, and the similarity to slugs became apparent. They come in all sizes, they are hard to get rid of, they leave your fingers slimy if you touch them, and they make you sick if you swallow them.

The Great Slug Contest was held, and many people mailed in their slugs. The first "thank you's" go to those people whether their slugs are printed here or not. There were too many, as is always the case with slugs.

There are other important "thank you's."

Editing, layout, typing and moral support were given in quantity and with love by Cathy Brown, Helen Budlong, Connie Eden, Beth Griffin, Gerry Toms, and Wanda Young.

An extra hug goes to Cathy Brown, who, when I would put my head on the desk and say *aggh,* offered a new idea and a lot of encouragement. Most of the time we laughed out loud at slugs that had become humorous instead of hurtful.

This new expanded edition has been put together with lots of assistance from Karen Erickson, Mary Fulton and Dolly Small.

Cover art by Jackie Phillips and Cynthia MacIsacc

The illustrations without identification in this book are by Steve McKinstry.

1

TABLE OF CONTENTS

"When a simpleton abused him, Buddha listened in silence; but when the man had finished, Buddha asked him, 'Son, if a man declined to accept a present made to him, to whom would it belong?' The man answered, 'To him who offered it.'

"'My son,' said Buddha, 'I decline to accept your abuse, and request you keep it for yourself.'"

Will Durant, *The Story of Civilization*

4

PREFACE

The Slug Manual is a collection of some of the slugs I received while working in the Northwest. These slugs have often been a part of people's lives for years. As you read them, you might see some that at one time have hurt you, but that you have now learned to laugh at.

They have been compiled into this book to give you a chance to put criticisms where they belong. The temptation is to give them back to the owners, but the best option is burial.

This book contains most of the major slug categories, but you will immediately think of your own. We have not discussed, in the interests of space and time, home-baked slugs, quickie slugs, nosey slugs, therapy slugs, tell-trail slugs, insatiable slugs, little nippers or boomerangs.

The first edition of The Slug Manual was a product of the Community Service Committee. The CSC is a group of friends who volunteer their time to help answer the requests of those who write to us for resources, information or counselors. Slugs were contributed by the Northwest community. This second edition is a product of Inner Cosmos Publishing.

Enjoy this book: use it to let go of old slugs and sidestep new ones. Pass it on to friends with love, and remember to take good care of yourself.

Jennifer James, Ph.D.
Seattle, 1984

When I was young I ate a slug ──────────────
Fed me by father and mother.
So many came to me after that
I didn't know one from another.

Some were slim and some were fat
And some were dressed to kill.
Some were so small they couldn't be seen
And some were the shape of a pill.

Brothers, sisters, cousins, and friends,
All had slugs to dish out.
I ate them all, like a pig in a stall
'til I came down with self-image gout.

'Tis a painful thing, I said to myself
No more of these will I eat.
I think I'll give myself a break
And swear off this horrible meat.

So I wrapped all the slugs in a lovely box
And sent them off C.O.D.
Said a cryptic note I had placed inside
THEY NO LONGER BELONG TO ME!

William Eickmeyer

'Constructive' Criticism?
There's No Such Animal

Your standards for you are too high.
Their evaluation of you is too low.

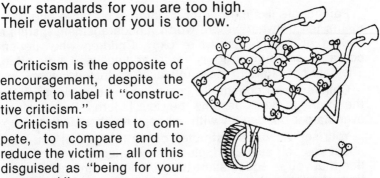

Criticism is the opposite of encouragement, despite the attempt to label it "constructive criticism."

Criticism is used to compete, to compare and to reduce the victim — all of this disguised as "being for your own good."

A lot of people cannot tell the difference between criticism and encouragement. Criticism tears people down, encouragement builds them up.

Criticism

"Mom, I got three A's on my report card!" "Well what about the other grades, why didn't you get all A's?"

"Dad, I mowed the lawn and I even put the lawn mower away!" "Well, did you wipe off the blades first, I'll bet you forgot that again, you're so careless."

"Look Dad, I just put together my first model airplane all by myself." "I can see you did it without help, it's a mess. There is glue all over everything. I could do better than this when I was half your age."

Encouragement

"Mom, I got three A's on my report card!" "That's wonderful, I know you've worked hard." (later that week) "I'm very proud of you and your grades, you'll do better each time because you know how to study."

"Dad, I mowed the lawn and I even put the lawn mower away." "Thank you son, you really are an asset to this family. We all appreciate your help. The lawn looks great! I forgot to mention the importance of cleaning the blades off when you finish, let's go and do that together now."

"Look Dad, I just put together my first model airplane all by myself." "You put this together all by yourself, congratulations. This is a really good start on building models. I see you had some trouble with the glue, that was hard for me too when I first started building models. It gets easier each time. I'll show you some of the tricks I learned."

Parents are like mirrors for children, their faces and comments tell us what we are worth. Encouragement instills a feeling of confidence, we're okay. Children who are encouraged and supported try harder and succeed more often. They are not afraid to make mistakes so they do more.

Children who constantly see failure and disapproval on their parents faces assume they are failures. Some will try even harder but usually with unhappy results. Most give up.

Your self-view is constructed of the things that you learn about yourself as a child, plus the experiences and information that you've added since then. We learn through observation of adults who care for us and through the ways they treat us.

If they are anxious about the world, we assume there are "things" to be anxious about. If they find fault with us, we assume we are at fault. We are in no position to argue.

Think back over your own experiences as a child and as an adult. Think about the criticisms that still sting even years later. You will understand on a personal level the power of criticism. There are many books that deal with re-building your sense of self if you were raised by highly critical parents. A good one is *Celebrate Yourself* by Dorothy Briggs.

Our sense of self has a lot to do with whether we are successful or not. If you feel you are not valuable you may not allow yourself to be successful. You will always assume any success you have is luck instead of your own hard work. Children whose accomplishments are discounted by their parents often spend their lifetime discounting their adult achievement. Check yourself, check those inner voices. See where the negative thoughts come from.

When you define success for yourself, can you choose a time in your life when you felt the most comfortable? What age was — or will be — the happiest for you?

The successful people in Gail Sheehy's book, *Pathfinders,* reveal that their happiest time wasn't youth, but the 60's for men, 70's for women. That's the opposite of what many of us believe.

These successful individuals were in control of their lives. They were free from much of the criticism that had been a part of their personal interactions.

Perfectionism

Reaching for the stars, perfectionists may end up clutching air. They suffer from mood disorder, troubled relationships and stress. They may even achieve less than others.

— David Burns

One of the results of constant criticism is a belief that love comes only to those who are perfect. The people who believe this end up with a mental illness called perfectionism. They feel that only when they have established perfect order and control over everything then they will be loved. Since perfection is an *illusion* they are forever disappointed and frustrated. They are very difficult people to live with.

The perfectionist wants the house perfect. It should look as though you moved out or sealed it in plastic. They cannot recognize that life is an ongoing process, that change is constant. They want the house perfect, the kitchen counter clean, a place for everything and everything in it's place. They would be happier if the other members of the family would just become neat pieces of furniture to be put on display. The perfectionist also wants the yard perfect, the car perfect, the dog perfect and everything at work perfect. They can even feel irritation over the condition of the neighbor's lawn. "Why oh why can't everyone live up to their high standards?"

Perfectionists care more for order than for people. They establish their worth only through control and score keeping. Their families are part of the score they hope to show the world and, of course, their never satisfied parents.

I have a friend who is in his forties. He has an older brother who is a doctor. His parents have always reminded him that he should have gone to college and been like his brother. These reminders have never stopped even though John, my friend, is very successful at his work.

Recently, his father had an eightieth birthday so John gave him a scholarship to the local community college. He said, "Dad, you've always wanted me to go to school. I thought if it was that important to you, you should go." His father immediately understood and said, "John I'm sorry I've criticised you and compared you to your brother." John's mother yelled from the kitchen, "John, we only want you to be the best you can be!" With some parents it never ends so you have to make peace with yourself.

The world is full of people who establish their worth by secret comparison and overt criticism.

9

The chickens in the yard understand the pecking order only when they are pecked. The peckers usually are individuals who were reared on conditional love — the parenting philosophy that holds that if a child cannot perform to a certain standard, he will by unloved and rejected. A child cannot debate the merits of the expectations presented to him or refute the criticism. So he learns to flinch at his own inadequacy and to avoid mistakes.

He becomes driven by his fear of being unloved. It follows him the rest of his life.

Parents who never seem satisfied with their children's accomplishments rear children who never are satisfied themselves.

Thus, the perfectionist has a shaky foundation that requires constant comparison and pursuit of the illusion of "being perfect."

An internal voice always reminds him that no matter how well he does anything, there always is a twinge of failure and the comment, "You could have done better."

Think of criticizers and perfectionists as people with an overabundance of something that we all know about here in the Northwest.

A bucket of slugs.

Some people need wheelbarrows to carry their slugs around.

I once met a perfectionist who needed a U-haul trailer.

They hope to give their slugs to others, which they think will make them feel better.

It doesn't work.

You only can be "perfect" by comparison, and therefore it requires reducing others. In a marriage, it's like punching holes in the heart of your relationship with a single-hole punch. It takes a while, but eventually the love falls apart.

The healthy pursuit of excellence, the genuine pleasure of meeting high standards, is often confused with perfectionism.

Perfectionism is based on a painful illusion, the illusion of personal perfectibility, people measured entirely by production or accomplishment.

Perfectionists lose sight of quality of life in their measurement of quantity. Order takes precedence over relationships. Their expectations are more important than acceptance and love. They can only see perfect and imperfect, so they are unable to enjoy any activity or person that would leave them in between.

Perfect performance becomes confused with perfect love. They are never satisfied. They never really feel safe or loved.

Sometimes perfectionists give up and become total failures. Some feel inadequate, but try to conceal it by demanding perfection from others. Some procrastinate, afraid to make mistakes. Some choose suicide to avoid the inevitable failure to maintain the illusion.

Recognize perfection as an illusion, not a desirable way to live. Don't confuse it with excellence. Enjoy your successes, laugh at your failures and learn from them.

There are lots of ways to cure the problem of perfectionism once you recognize the symptoms and want to change. One of the best descriptions of how to reduce perfectionism is from the book *INSTANT RELIEF: The Encyclopedia of Self-Help* by Tom Greening and Dick Hobson. They list the following possible ways to make your life, and the life of those around you, a more pleasant experience:

- *Rediscover yourself as more than the sum of your actions and products. Perfectionism is a way of living that overidentifies you with what you do and produce. It distracts from your awareness of what you are: an ordinary human, with all the inevitable mortal flaws. We seek love and fear rejection. We are curious and creative, but often stumble and bungle. Those people in your life whose love is worth having will love and value you for yourself, not for the perfect "display image" you've been trying to project.*

- *Recognize perfection as an unattainable ideal, not a possible or even desirable way for human beings to live. We need to make mistakes in order to learn and to grow. Don't waste your time stewing over errors or even failures. Look for what they have to teach you and move on.*

- Strive for excellence, and when you do a good job let yourself enjoy it. The antidote to perfectionism is not to give up striving for improvement but to learn to accept yourself as a living, growing, imperfect — but improving and well-intentioned — individual.
- Repeat to yourself a new motto to replace the old one. "Anything worth doing is worth doing badly." If we care about doing something, we ought to be willing to do it for its own sake, not to demonstrate how well we can do it. Tackling complex and difficult projects with real significance necessitates suffering through times of uncertainty, frustration, and failure. In art, music, science, teaching, sports, and other creative spheres of life, excellence is reached only in specific fleeting moments. Tasks accomplished with too much control lose the human quality of creative struggle that makes them exciting. Some artists say they never finish a painting — they abandon it.

    Stress your accomplishments in your mind. Stop listening to your overdemanding, never-satisfied inner judge. Do not keep score of your failures or mistakes. Do not exaggerate the difference between what you achieve and the goal you are striving toward.
- Look at the specific ways in which you are a perfectionist. Do you focus on looks, work, housekeeping? Under what circumstances are you likely to behave in a perfectionist manner? Are you competing? Are you compensating for some real or imagined flaw in yourself?
- Imagine not doing something perfectly. What are the external consequences (not your internal responses)? If there are none — as is likely — look at the self-destructive nature of your perfectionism. Look carefully at your internalized unrealistic expectations. See that they are, in fact, enemies, not helpful friends. Begin to revise, lower, or drop these expectations.

    Don't get hooked on someone else's standards. If your parents are never content with what you do, recognize that they have a need to be discontented — not that you have never done anything worthwhile. Identify your own values. Strive to satisfy your own needs. If it's really more important to you to develop your photographic skill than to have the best-trimmed lawn on the block, don't be pressured by your neighbor's disapproval. A nightclub singer got fed up with the perfectionistic demands she and others placed on her, quit, and went to college, where she enjoyed learning new things in an atmosphere she found more supportive.

- Refrain from self-criticism and from harsh criticism of others. Work at accepting everyone's efforts graciously and positively. As an exercise, keep track of how often you criticize yourself and others (both internally and out loud). Use a golf-score counter to tick off each instance. Now, reward yourself for reducing this negative behavior. Give yourself points for the actual number of reductions in negative thoughts and for rejecting such thoughts when they do occur. Do something nice for yourself each time you earn five or ten points.
- Work at becoming less competitive. Stop comparing yourself to others as if you were always involved in an important rivalry. Praise yourself for your real achievements and positive qualities. Don't dump on yourself because someone else does something better than you do. There is no absolute "number one" in life. We're all working, learning, growing, and changing in our relationships to each other.
- Laugh. Make jokes. Look at the funny side to life's dramas. Very few things in life are so serious that there isn't some opportunity for humor. Recognize and accept the comic aspects of trying and failing. So much is really beyond our control that there is ample room for humor in the distance between what we want and what we get.
- Don't pass along your perfectionism to your kids. Praise and encourage them sincerely and appropriately. Let them know that you love them no matter how they perform. Give them opportunities to learn to make decisions and to take responsibility. Help them learn from mistakes without feeling ashamed or unacceptable. Show them that your love is not conditional on their being perfect. You may find that while you're concentrating on treating them generously and lovingly you're also learning to treat yourself with the same consideration.

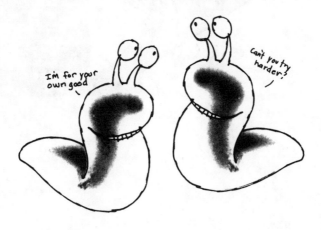

Slime pit

Criticism is like a slug. It's hard to handle because it's slimy. If you are feeling 'sluggish,' no doubt someone has 'slugged' you in the tummy and made it hard to move ahead.

What Can You Do?

What can you do when you're 34 — not 4 — and someone hands you a slug?

You could look at it, recognize that it's not yours and either drop it or hand it back. If the slugs that you're handed look like they belong to you, then someone has reduced your sense of self and it's time to get help re-evaluating.

When you put the slug down or hand it back, you'll still feel the slime on your fingers, but that's better than holding on to the whole thing.

There are a lot of ways to unload someone else's slug:

- You can ask such people, "Why do you want to give me a slug?" That is like asking them why they want to hurt you. They won't be able to give you the true answer, which is, "Because I've got so many slugs that they're making me sick." They'll also realize you're not an easy victim and take their slugs elsewhere. They might get angry, because people who have a lot of slugs to unload are afraid. Fear usually hides itself in anger and irritation. sometimes they'll switch to tiny slugs, hoping you won't notice. They'll also use slug sandwiches, two nice comments with a slug in between.

  My mother used to put ground liver in my orange juice so I'd be healthy. I always thought something was in the glass, but didn't know until I got to the bottom. Little slugs are like that. Give them back.

- If you have a strong sense of your worth, you usually can just throw the slug away and wash your hands. But it's important to recognize that you've been given a slug — or you might swallow it. You can always tell when you've been given a slug because it's like being punched or stuck with a pin.

- Sometimes just flinching or saying "Oh!" will help. Let them know you noticed the slug.

  When at a party, for example, if your spouse or a friend criticizes you, just go "Oh!" as if you were hurt — then go on with the conversation. Don't refer to the comment.

  If someone asks what's wrong. Tell them you just felt a pin prick.

- One family stopped slugs around the dinner table by using a bell. Whenever grandfather criticized someone they rang the bell. He realized he couldn't get away with it anymore.

- A great strategy (if you have a sense of humor) is to agree with the criticizer, which gives him the slug back. It eliminates the power of the slug by disintegrating it, just as though you had sprinkled it with salt. Here are some examples of how to return slugs:

Slug: You've gained weight, dear. Aren't you about 20 pounds overweight?
You: Yes. Actually, it's closer to 25. Terrible, isn't it?
Slug: Aren't you going to do anything about it?
You: Probably not...I'm just going to be fat for a while.

Slug: Aren't those pimples on your face?
You: Yes. There are 42. I bet there'll be more tomorrow.
Slug: They sure are ugly.
You: Oh, they're worse than ugly. I've probably got terminal acne. Do you want me to turn out the lights?

One woman's husband used to give her a list of things before he left for work in the morning that he wanted done in the house. If she didn't finish everything, he would become angry and withdraw his love. She was so sure that she was incompetent that she ran faster and faster trying to please him.

But the lists kept getting longer and more detailed, until she was spending most of her time trying to keep out of trouble. Sometimes she was supposed to do things that weren't even on the list because "any intelligent person would have know it."

The problem wasn't her husband's expectations. It was the woman's need to prove her competence. He, however, had made an investment in proving that she was not as competent as he. He wanted control.

She went to a counselor because she didn't like herself — or her husband. The counselor suggested she give up trying to be perfect, that she lose the lists, make mistakes, buy the wrong things. Her husband eventually decided that his wife was, indeed, incompetent and gave up giving her lists.

She regained control of her own life. And then she could love herself — and her husband — again.

Can you be loved if you're not perfect?

- If you cannot refuse the slug or throw it away or give it back, you may end up swallowing it. What happens when you eat slugs? You get sick.

Look back over the past week and evaluate the number of slugs you've swallowed or handed back.

Who gives you slugs? What do you do with them?

If you cannot remember, begin a new list today and keep track of where your slugs are coming from.

It's easy to recognize the big ones. But the little, tiny ones require you to keep in touch with your stomach. When someone hands you a well-dressed slug, only your stomach will know. It will tighten in fear that you're going to swallow it.

Sometimes you won't identify the slug until a few hours later. But as soon as you do, unload it. Keep track of who hands you the most slugs. If you cannot avoid that person, start working on handing his slugs back. (A book to help you with this is *Celebrate Yourself,* by Dorothy Briggs.)

Where do these slugs come from?

Why do perfectionists push them around in wheelbarrows?

Why do we swallow them?

We repeat old patterns that are familiar. Feelings and actions that are familiar feel safe, even when they're negative. If you were given a lot of slugs as a child and dutifully swallowed them, you will look for close companions who will make you feel at home. When you meet someone who doesn't hand you slugs, you might feel that something is missing in the relationship.

The key issue, if you have trouble evaluating criticism, or if you are the source of your critical voice, is to ask yourself: What do I see?

Get out your notebook again and list your good qualities. List at least 10.

If you cannot find 10, ask a friend to contribute to the list. Add one new quality to the list every day until you have at least 25.

You may be going around with an empty self-esteem cupboard. It is time to start putting things on the shelf, one at a time.

Check your internal cupboard. How many good things are on the shelf?

When did you last add some?

Who is taking them out?

THE
INTERNAL CUPBOARD

Slug Trail 1

Slug Sandwich

The slug sandwich is a combination of two compliments with a slug in between. "What a nice dress: such a great color. It's a shame that you look so sallow in purple." (The dress, of course, is purple.) People often suspect they are slug-givers, so they try to slip them in so you won't notice, or at least be too confused to catch them. You can always tell a slug sandwich by the fact that your stomach tightens though you are not sure why.

We are often tempted to give slug sandwiches, or the sugar-coated pill, to children. "You've done so well at this, John, but you didn't clean this corner or that corner." A better way to handle this problem is to say that he did a fine job, then wait until the next time you assign the job and add extra information about cleaning corners. Most compliments are quickly negated if they are next to a slug. Sometimes the slug hurts more because the compliment opened the person up.

Try to separate your compliments from any negatives you have to mention. If you are an employer or evaluator you will have to criticize because the employee or client has made a contract with you to do work or get feedback. Under other circumstances think carefully about whether you need to mention the negative. Usually noting the positive, "That's a good start," and adding more information later works better.

Try out these slug sandwiches and see if you can think of any you've heard or used.

In 1971, I moved from Ohio to Wilmington, Delaware, to live with a man I planned to marry as soon as my divorce came through. One day my sister called to tell me that one of her friends lived there also and that I should give her a call. At that time it wasn't as popular as it is now to live with someone without the benefit of marriage, so I told my sister I was uncomfortable letting anyone know my circumstances, and would rather not call her friend. "Oh, that's okay, she's a whore," she said in a tone that said you are too.

The following was said by a 53-year-old divorced man to a widow on her first date after 32 years of marriage: "I used to see some of the guys in the department with their fat wives, and I always wondered how they could love somebody like that! But now I've met you and I know it is the personality of the person."

It was presented in such a way as to make one think it was meant to be a compliment. Whatever...it was cruel.

Father-in-law slugs:
Wife: "How do you like Michael's singing, Daddy?"
Father-in-law: "Well, I know why he sings so well. He's got legs like a canary!"

My neighbor telephoned me one day to tell me how much she liked my hair, which I had recently "frosted." She went on to say how much younger it made me look, etc. I felt like a million dollars when I hung up the phone. A few minutes later she called back to continue the conversation about my hair. She said even her husband had remarked how nice I looked since frosting my hair. "In fact," she said, "we both agree that the lighter color is much more flattering against your skin as it doesn't make your pores appear so large."

The therapy slug: A group member asked the therapist what strategies he used to fight depression. He left us all slack-jawed when he answered, "I find helping people with their problems helps me, but, of course, you don't have that option."

"That's a great looking dress, dear. Too bad they didn't have your size."

"I really like that dress. If you hang onto it, it will probably come back in style."

Upon returning from a really good party late at night, husband says to wife, "Honey, you really looked good tonight in that dress, even though your slip was showing."

When I thanked a neighbor for the vase she sent me for a wedding present, she commented, "I think it's quite ugly, and I didn't want to look at it any more."

Many years later, I invited a charming neighbor and her children to have coffee with me. I had noticed when visiting in her home that among her nice furnishings were a pair of matching lamps very much like some I had recently purchased. I could hardly believe my ears when she said, "I have lamps like those. I can't wait to find something in good taste so that I can get rid of them."

I can recognize slugs that are disguised as questions such as:

"You look so nice when you dress properly. Are you wearing a bra?"

"I love apples in my coleslaw. Do you ever put apples in yours?"

"I sleep so well in a good bed. Do you plan to get a new one soon?"

I was passing by my boss at work. My boss says, "I like those pretty overalls you're wearing, too bad you don't have a body to go with it."

Home-Baked Slugs

Sick slug: "This homemade soup tastes so good. I'm feeling better already."

"It should taste good. I've been working on it in the kitchen all day while you've been lying in bed."

Susan Dixon

Since listening to you and with work on my part, I've gotten control of a long-term obesity problem and have been able to stay on a reducing diet with good results. Feeling good about myself, I made a beautiful new outfit, in the color that the *Color Me Beautiful* book says is perfect for me, turquoise. I was dining in a waterfront restaurant with my tall, handsome, college-aged son and went into the restroom. As I was touching up my lipstick, a well-dressed woman turned to me and said how wonderful the color was for me. I felt really glowing inside and thanked her for the compliment. The woman responded, "I, for one, will be so glad when turquoise comes back in style."

"You have a nice figure for someone your age."
"Your hair looks nice. It's really something what hairdressers can do with hair."

Best-dressed slug: "That's certainly an interesting dress! I saw one just like it at K-Mart on sale! Where did you get it?" Reply: "At K-Mart on sale."

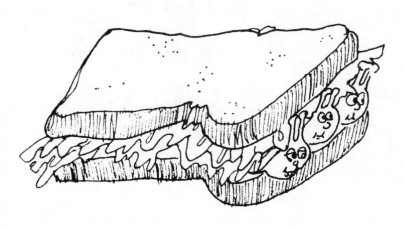

Susan Dixon

Slug Trail 2

Mother-In-Law and Step-Parent Slugs

These can include fathers-in-law and various other relatives. The criticisms are based on a competitive model. "You couldn't possibly be good enough to be part of our family," or "I am the woman/mother in his life, and he will always prefer me over you."

The only way to handle these types of slugs is to either ignore them or agree with them. "You are a much better _____ than I; poor George has to live with me." Never, never be drawn into actual competition. There is no way your spouse can choose between you and his or her parent without some problems.

Do the same when your children bring home grandparents' comments. "Grandfather is probably right. I am a spendthrift." Your children will make up their own minds anyway, and you'll keep them out of the middle. Grandpa will have lost most of his power when the kids tell him that you agree.

Other categories of in-law slugs include divorce and step-parent slugs. The basic reason for the criticism is always the same. "I'm afraid you might be better than me, so I'll tell everyone you are worse." Stay out of competition, and keep the kids out.

Let's say your ex-husband tells your son that you are ruining his life by demanding he pay child support. You can either ignore it and gently tell your son that these are adult matters and you won't bother him about it, or agree that you are trying to ruin his father's life. Your son will quickly see the humor and that he cannot play you off against his father. It also releases him from being in the middle because your ex-husband will eventually give up passing criticism through the children.

It is important to remember that these slugs can also go from daughter or son-in-law to mother or father-in-law or step-parent. Check how you handle your feelings of competition and whether jealousy leads you to criticize.

Here are a few of the best in-law, step-parent slugs:

Step-mother slug: My step-mother was invited to my grand-parents' for Sunday dinner. She relished every mouthful and then commented, "Oh Annie, that was wonderful. Chicken is cheap now, isn't it." Now in our family whenever someone hands out a criticism and we notice, someone says, "Chicken is cheap," and we all crack up.

Mother: "A loving daughter wouldn't see her father if he and I split up."

Mother-in-law to son-in-law:
My husband and I were discussing the care that must be taken to insure that no grandchildren would fall into the deep end of the new swimming pool being installed in my mother's front yard. My mother quipped to my husband, "You went off the deep end when you married Gretchen."

Mother-in-law slug: "Now that Tom has remarried and is so happy, he doesn't need to take drugs anymore as he did when he was married to you."

When we informed my husband's folks that we were engaged to be married, his mother's only comment was, "What color is your wedding dress going to be?"
Being the demure young bride-to-be, I replied, "It will be white; I don't look good in stripes or polka dots."

My mother-in-law would look at our two little boys. "Johnny is so handsome; he looks exactly like his father. Poor Jimmy looks like you."

After the first meal served to in-laws, my mother-in-law said, "I saw some winesap apples in your fruit bowl. I hope you didn't make this pie with that type of apple—I simply can't abide winesap apples."
Reply (as I wisked the pie from under her nose): "Isn't that thoughtful of you to tell me. Now I have an extra piece for lunch tomorrow."

During Christmas, I visited with my sister by telephone. She was telling me about her son's resolution to stop drinking. She said her mother-in-law was visiting, and her son said, "Well, Grandma, it has been a year since I've had a drink of anything alcoholic."
Response: "Well, now you drink too much Pepsi."

My 36-year-old aunt received this slug from her 6-year-old daughter after asking her to bring her sister's coat out to the car:
Megan: "Do you ever think of me as Cinderella?"
Mother: "No."
Megan: "Well I sure think of you as the old ugly step-mother."

My sister's mother-in-law always looked down on me for being a cocktail waitress. When my sister told her I had changed jobs and was now working at her favorite apparel store, she said, "Oh, I didn't know Nordstrom's had a restaurant."

My mother-in-law was very proud of her ample proportions and called attention to them frequently. One day she said to me, "How did you ever manage to keep your bosom so small?"

My daughter Sarah was born with a cleft lip and palate. When my mother-in-law came to see her for the first time she said, "She sure doesn't look like anybody on our side of the family." (My daughter looks very much like my husband).

Mother-in-law (excitedly): "I finally found out why your sister-in-law dislikes you so. You laugh too much."
Response: "Ha, ha, ha, ha...

During our first months of marriage, we had both sets of parents over for New Year's Day and served a standing rib roast beef dinner. My mother-in-law said to my mother, "I used to worry that none of my girls could cook, but I see your daughter doesn't know how either."

I have my MS in Foods; my mother has an MS in Home Ec.

On the occasion of my mother-in-law's first look at my new baby, she said, "Oh, good. I see she doesn't have her eyes too close together."

Pause. "Not that your eyes are that close together, dear."

—Susan Dixon

Slug Trail 3

Tiny Slugs

Tiny slugs are hard to hear but easy to feel. They are very small slights or insults that gradually accumulate. We realize that we are uncomfortable around a particular person, but aren't sure why. We wonder if we aren't being too sensitive to his brand of humor of helpful comments. Tiny slugs are like the following:

"You look much better in dark colors that don't add weight."

"The meal was just fine, don't worry."

"My son never used to be so tired."

"That was an adequate job you did. Thank you."

"I hope you'll help. You are the only one who has the time."

"I enjoy your daughter. Every group needs followers as well as leaders."

Tiny slugs are sometimes referred to as a lack of tact. The usual emotion behind them is competition. People want to be very careful and subtle, but they still want to put you down in their great scoring record.

You can recognize tiny slugs by the little pin prick you feel when you get one. Sometimes you look like a pin cushion before you say, "Oh! That's it! That's why I feel bad."

Tiny slugs need to be ignored, avoided, or handed back just like their more obvious, bigger, slimier cousins. A stomach or heart full of tiny slugs hurts as much as a stomach or heart with one large slug.

List some tiny slugs. See if you can catch them.

Friend, at a party: "You look great. I've ALWAYS loved that dress."

The Jennifer James Slug:
Me: "Honey, how about sending a slug to J.J."
Wife: "No, I don't want J.J. to know what a dumb ass of a husband I have..."
Me: "Well, I guess I will send one slug to the J.J. Show."
Wife: "I don't think you should. You never get things right."
Me: "Well, I could think of a good slug."
Wife: "But, Honey, that takes brains."
Me: "Look at it this way. If we win, we will get a dinner with Jennifer."
Wife: "Then Jennifer will know what a stupid husband I have."
Me: "Well, I guess I'll just have to work this out by myself."
Wife: "See how insensitive and selfish you are? You never include me in any of your plans..."

"What do you expect to amount to? Don't you have any plans to make something of your life?"
"Set your sights a little higher, dear."
"Don't tough it. You'll make it worse."
"Here's a good book on the subject. It's written so simply, even YOU should be able to understand it."
"Congratulations on accomplishment. You finally made it!"

Mother-daughter slug: "You really keep a nice house. Everything is so neat. But you must remember to dust your toilet paper holders. People notice things like that, you know."

Left-handed compliment for my meat loaf dinner complete with homemade bread and pie: "My, you're a fine, economical cook."

Housekeeping slug: "My, look at all this dirt you have in this corner."
Response: "Oh, dear, I can live in a little dirt as I intend to die in dirt."

Novice cook slug: "Well, that was filling."

I love the way you entertain! It's so casual.

Slug Trail 4

Time Release Slugs

This is a particularly insidious slug. You don't notice it when you first get it. Then, later, it begins to explode in your stomach. Some of these slugs have been known to continue releasing pricks for weeks and even years.

Examples are hard to come by because they are so subtle. "You should have changed your hair years ago. It looks nice now." Or, "I saw your husband in a bar with your friend. It's nice he knows how to enjoy himself."

The only way to handle these slugs is to recognize them right away. Then you can either opt for the compliment and forget the rest, or you can subtly get more information, or you can stay away from that person in the future.

A plastic surgeon, checking my eldest son's recovery from surgery, saw my youngest son for the first time. The boy was then two years old. The doctor, whose business, after all, is faces and bone structure, said to me, "How did YOU ever manage to have such a beautiful child?"

I found out from my sister-in-law that I was making my baby's bath water too hot. This prompted the following from my mother-in-law: "What are you trying to do? Cook my baby?"

Mother-in-law's reply when thanked for a gift at Christmas: "Oh, do you like the bathrobe? I'm so glad. Marvin didn't like it on me."

During the first meeting with her future daughter-in-law, the mother went down the hall with her son and said in a loud voice: "Son, why don't you go out with a small, cute girl?"

Mother: "You were so pretty in high school."
Daughter: "Why, thank you."
Mother: "...and you were so friendly. You always had a smile for everyone. The boys liked you so much. You were so popular with all of them. That's because you weren't a threat to them. Boys hate brainy girls, you know."

The amnesic slug:
Mother to her young child: "I've forgotten more than you will ever know."

"So you've read one page — a little knowledge is a dangerous thing."

Our son had a few dates with Sally and one day brought her home to meet us. In the awkward moments following the introductions we were standing there looking at one another when Sally blurted out, "How in the world did two such short, fat people have a tall, slender son?"

As woman leaves costly beauty shop, male owner bellows: "Darling, when you came in you looked like 1965 — now you look like 1982."

One of my sister's co-workers, who had recently had nose surgery, was complaining that she did not like the shape of her nose. A person who did not know her before the surgery asked what her nose had looked like. She struggled to describe it and then, after a pause, looked around the room and pointed to my sister and said, "Oh, it was like Darlyne's nose!"

Once when my husband was in grade school, his class was preparing to go down the halls Christmas caroling. As they left the room, the teacher turned to my husband and said, "And can you HUM?"

Boss to employee: "This office looks really nice the way you've fixed it up. DON'T GET USED TO IT."

Upon my receiving a compliment on the dinner I had just served, my sister-in-law said, "Anyone can be a domestic."

After I had been complemented on an artistic endeavor, my sister-in-law said, "Wanda works well with her hands. I use my head."

Ever since early childhood I have adored music. There was not much music around our house — my parents did not play or sing. I used to sit glued to the TV whenever I could find anything musical.

When an opportunity was announced for students to take band in junior high, I was excited at the prospect of learning to play the French horn (furnished by the school). When I asked my parents for the required permission, my mother said, "No, I don't want you to take it. Music is for people who have talent, and it would mean money wasted down the line for you."

Second-hand slug: When I was in my twenties, a boyfriend took me to meet his mother. Later he told me she said to him, "She's very nice, but she's so PLAIN." I felt very hurt because she confirmed my secret fear that I wasn't special. I still hurts fifteen years later.

I still remember a slug handed me over 42 years ago. I was a shy, sensitive teenager just beginning to make the dating scene. My very new boyfriend received the following note from his very recent ex-girlfriend:

Dear Jack,

No hard feeling. Dorothy is a very nice girl.

In fact, her niceness more than makes up for her lack of looks.

Love forever,

Mary Louise

College assignment officer: "Well, go ahead and apply for the job. You've always been lucky."

Mother to child in carpool: "How old were you when your nose was broken?" (The child's nose had never been broken.)

The world-threat slug: "Wait until the world gets a hold of you."

Husband-wife slug: My husband and I were both being treated by the same psychotherapist. I had just begun to have complete confidence, respect, and admiration for the therapist when my husband said, "Dr. _____ says you are a thorn in my side."

One new friend to the other upon parting, "Great to have met you. I don't care *what* they say about you—I think you're all right!"

As I met a friend of my future husband, Roy, she took my hand, examined my ring and said, "Oh, that's exactly like the ring Roy gave Marge!" (his ex-wife).

While I was fixing a special dinner (pastry stuffed with meat and vegetables, which when all spread out looks rather complicated), the mother of one of my friends came to pick up her daughter's friends. She is a mother who works outside the home full time. She watched me for several minutes and then said, "Well, I've never been a little Susie Homemaker."

At a wedding reception, from a friend of the groom's family: "We always thought your husband would choose someone special. We're glad you're just an ordinary person."

Mother to daughter slug: (In reference to the fact that my husband is often unemployed) "Your father and I always tried so hard to take care of you. I wish you had someone to take care of you now." This statement came in spite of the fact that I am a well-paid executive.

Slug Trail 5

Well-Dressed Slugs

These glamour slugs are known also as constructive criticism. Picture our slimy friend in a tuxedo or covered with glitter. This is a slug usually accompanied by one of these phrases: "I hope you don't mind if I'm honest." "This is for your own good." "Please don't get mad at me, but..." "I always speak my mind." "I'll be candid with you." Then they insult you.

You end up confused because you are supposed to admire them for their honesty and appreciate their concern for you while you try to recover from the punch you've received in the stomach.

Try to complete this phrase and you may remember some well-dressed slugs in your past: "If I didn't care for you, I wouldn't tell you that _____."

The following are a selection of glitter slugs.

— ONE OF THE BEST DRESSED SLUGS —

I heard this slug from my mother to my father frequently when I was nine or ten years old and felt the ricocheting wounds myself. To understand this slug, you must know that my father was quite bald and not the typical image of success, despite great kindness and generosity of spirit. My mother would rub my thick brush-cut hair and say, "THIS is my mink coat."

Mother-daughter slug: "Do you know what's wrong with you??? You can't take criticism!"

We moved into a beautiful new home, but the builder had left the landscaping to us. As a result, I donned my oldest work clothes and spent 4 or 5 hours a day, rain or shine, picking weeds and rocks out of the mud trying to get some semblance of order out of the mess. One day I took off to go shopping and was on my way to the car, when my neighbor stopped me and asked if I had a new outfit on. After I said no, she said, "Oh, it's so much more attractive than the outfit you've been wearing to work in the yard."

"A new skirt? That looks like material you would use to upholster a chair."
Reply: "If this looks like chair material, I'd better sit down and find someone to sit on my lap."

Aunt: "I see your boyfriend bought you a very expensive watch for Christmas. You must be awfully good in bed."
Niece: "I guess you could say that is one of my qualities. I see Uncle Bill bought you a Timex."

In a flower show that both my mother and I entered, I did well but she did not. While I was showing my ribbons to a dear friend in her presence, my mother remarked, "No wonder you won so many ribbons: you entered everything."

"Oh, you're left-handed. I hear there's a school that you can go to now to get over that."

Remark made by someone looking at a picture of me when I was eighteen:

"You were much better looking before you got false teeth!"

After several months of dating my ex-husband and quite a few times in bed together, my ex-husband propped his head up on his arm after having sex and said, "I think you are really getting involved with me and I want you to know that I don't think I can fall in love with you because you really aren't that pretty." Can you believe I married him anyway?

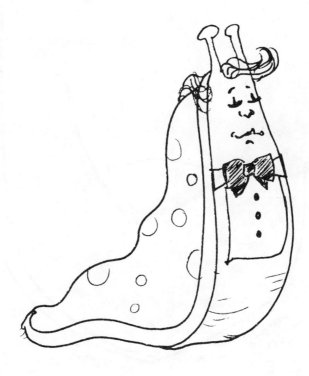

Susan Dixon

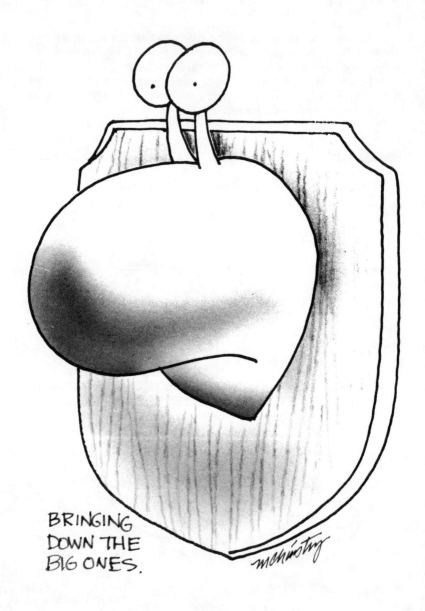

BRINGING
DOWN THE
BIG ONES.

Slug Trail 6

Heirloom Slugs

Criticisms are often passed down through a family from generation to generation. If your mother or father called you a particular name you will be tempted to repeat it. I remember being called "Jellybags" whenever my mother thought I was envious of someone or jealous. Every so often that name still comes to my lips in reference to my own children. I have to remind myself to suppress it.

What names or labels can you remember from your past?

Do you still use these names for yourself and others?

What names might you be passing on? "Dummy"? "Stupid"? "Selfish"? "Troublemaker"?

If we call someone by a label long enough he begins to believe it. Long after the information is proven to be untrue, he is unable to stop thinking of himself as "dumb" or "fat" or whatever he was called.

Heirloom slugs often refer to characteristics assumed to be passed down. "You are just like all the women in your family. You are all crabs." You are guilty through some historical connection that indicates you as part of the related group. Can you think of an heirloom slug that:

Lumps a group together regardless of their individual characteristics?

Uses other related people in the family to bolster the criticism?

Gives criticism by saying, "You've always been that way," or "I've been telling you to change for years."?

Sometimes heirloom slugs are a wonderful source of humor. They become a story that is passed down through a family. Here are some "old" slugs.

Informative slugs from my mother:
"Everyone is afraid of you."
"Nobody understands you."
"You're an emotional tyrant."
"You're cold." "You're selfish."
"You're too friendly with people."
"You're always trying to please people."
"You can't make it on your own."
"When you get through 'growing up' you'll be back."
"If you leave me you'll be giving up your spirituality."

A male driver who had rear-ended me would not give me the insurance information I requested. In a condescending tone, he said, "I'll be glad to discuss the accident with your husband." I smiled sweetly and said that would be fine as long as I could talk with his wife!

My brother lives in the East. He and I were reunited after a nineteen-year separation to attend the funeral of our father in the Midwest. After making the rounds of supportive friends and relatives, we made our dutiful call on Aunt Nell. When we were leaving, Aunt Nell said, "Just a minute, you two. I have something to say. Twelve years ago when your father retired, my son-in-law asked him if he could rent his property. Your father said, 'We'll see if we can make a deal...,' but then he rented to someone else. The whole community has been laughing at us ever since. Now explain why he would do that to us." I wish I were an artist. Can't you just see an angry slug with her little shovel, digging in the cemetery filled with little grave markers inscribed "Insults from 1902," "Insults from 1903," etc.?

After a very sticky divorce where I lost all my prized china and silver and other beautiful possessions that I took very good care of, I remarried and brought little of beauty or value to the new marriage. Shortly after our marriage, I was pleased to find that my husband's grandmother's silver was coming our way. When I expressed the fact that I would like to keep it neatly stored in the compartments designed for silver in my antique dry sink, my new husband exclaimed, "Do you think I'd let you take care of this silver? Then it would end up looking like the crap you have now." He proceeded to leave it loose in a box, in his closet where he is saving it for his daughter. (An eight year old who lives with her mother in California.)

The Love Slug

"You know I wouldn't say this if I didn't love you...."

I was standing at the bathroom mirror one evening at the tender age of 12 or 13, when my mother walked in and said, "Don't worry, honey. If your nose gets any bigger, we can have it fixed." Up until that point it had never even occured to me that my nose could be anything less than perfect (and it only took about ten years for me to again love my classically chiseled Roman Proboscis).

Brother to me: "You don't wear shoes. They're gunboats."
Brother to me: "Your legs look like fenceposts."
Mom to me: "You'll never have a pretty baby. You're such a plain Jane. All your brothers (16 of them) were pretty babies."

Family slugs:
Do you realize how much I *sacrificed* for you?
I stayed with your father just for you.

Mother-Daughter Slugs

After I shared my new job description with my mother, she said, "How did YOU ever get a job like that?"

"You don't need all those children—you're too busy *working* all day long to be a good mother to them. You ought to send them to me. I could give them what they need..."

Married daughter slugs:
"It's your fault my life is so miserable. You should have stopped me from *getting married*."
"When are you and Dad going to stop going away weekends and stay home and babysit like *you should*?
"So what if you helped us financially all those times and bought stuff for the kids? My neighbor's mother gives her money all the time."

Slug Trail 7

Overweight

This may be the single biggest category of slugs. We are all raised to be very conscious of our appearance, and yet everyone acts as if we don't care if we're insulted. The media points out daily the perfect body image, and it doesn't look anything like us.

People talk about what's wrong with us when we're children as if we don't exist. "Look at that nose; who's going to marry her?" "If he's short like Uncle John he'll be sorry." "Don't you think he takes after Marvin? I hope he turns out better." "She has terrible hair." "He has enormous feet; you know what they say about big feet, har, har." "She'd be so pretty if she'd lose some weight." "Hey, here comes the whale."

Patti Davis, Nancy Reagan's daughter, says that no matter how hard she tries she always leaves the house and finds out there's something wrong with the way she looks. There's a spot or a button missing, or she didn't do her hair right, or she has a pimple. She says her mother always looks perfect, but Patti hasn't figured out how to do it.

The hardest part of body image seems to be weight. We're always too thin or too fat, too tall or too short, too big here and too small there. Perfection will elude you forever unless you cover yourself in white cotton and ascend.

Mae West said, "Too much of a good thing is wonderful." But most of us understand that being overweight is a signal to others that we are vulnerable, and they go after us.

Try to unload all the body image slugs you've picked up along the way. Most of them have long since become irrelevant to your life and your values. Stand in front of a mirror and make a list. List all the things about your body that you don't like. That is an enemies' list because all those parts are going into the future with you. Take the list and figure out which parts on it you're going to change.

You can gain weight or lose weight, or cut your hair or curl it. You can get braces or have your nose fixed. Go over everything and decide carefully what you want to do. Finally, you'll have a list of parts you cannot change or don't want to spend the money, time or effort to change. Take each part on that list and put your hand on it. Say the following: "Part (nose, butt, etc.), I've let people insult you. I've sometimes joined in. You've been with me a long time and are going to be with me a long time. Part, I love you." Make friends with yourself, all the parts, and it will be easier to sidestep the slugs.

Husband: "You know, I think your thighs are getting even bigger."

Wife: "You know, I think you're right, Baldy." (It was the first time I had ever made reference to his thinning hair.)

After losing considerable weight and with a friend's encouragement, I took the risk and wore a pair of shorts. I started feeling pretty good about it, until my friend said, "Oh Jane, you really are much worse looking than I expected. If I were you I would go for some corrective surgery."

Over a period of months I lost 20 pounds by exercise and by a careful plan of dieting. As I was struggling, I gained 5 pounds back. My mother, who hadn't seen me for several months, without saying "Hello" or "How are you," said, "Getting a little fat, aren't you, honey?"

I said, "Gee, Mom, it's nice to see you, too."

"I don't know why YOU should have so much trouble sticking to a diet. I know both your parents, and they're both people with lots of will power!" This slug was from my doctor, who also told my son, "You have got to start eating better and build yourself up. Take about half your mother's food. She sure doesn't need it."

Grandmother to mother slug:

"Oh, you've got a new pants suit. You look like a barn in red."

"If you would just wear a little make-up you could be so pretty."

A friend of mine received this slug from a disliked relative: "I've never weighed this much in my life! I must weigh as much as you do!"

A devastating slug: "Oh, I see you've lost weight, haven't you?" Puffing proudly, I said, "Yes, isn't it great! I'm happy it shows."

"It really does show, but your face has gotten so thin, though, hasn't it?"

When I was in my teens, I was tall, well-developed and somewhat on the chunky side. I always wanted a dress with a full gathered skirt, which was in style at the time. My mother and I went shopping one day for a new dress. I found a lovely floral print with a full gathered skirt. I went into the dressing room and tried it on, excited with the prospect of owning such a stylish dress. I then modeled the dress for my mother. My mother's comment was, "Isn't that a lovely dress! It's a shame it makes you look like a bag of wheat with a string tied in the middle of it."

My grandmother is a real pro at slugging. She is 84 and still going strong at it. My niece invited a little friend, aged 8, to join several family members, including Grandma, for breakfast at a restaurant. My grandmother noticed that my niece's friend was eating quite fast. She said, loud enough for all to hear while directing her glance at the little guest, "Well, I guess we know who's going to have a weight problem when she grows up."

"Oh, I see you are doing the thing that you do best—eating again."

"You would be such a pretty girl if you would only quit eating."

"You're starting to look really good. Have you been dieting?"

"My step-daughter gave me a huge nightgown that I can't wear. It's so big I thought of you. You'll be able to fill it out."

"Even though you're overweight, you're solid fat, not sloppy fat."

"You used to have such a nice figure when you were younger. What happened?"

Mother-daughter slugs: I am a much larger woman than my mother, so I get things like, "I feel sorry for your brother. You have been a source of embarrassment to him."

"My hands are so huge I feel ashamed of them." Then, looking at my much larger hands, she says, "I'm glad your hands are useful."

Slug from Mom:
"That dress looks nice, dear, if you don't gain any more weight."

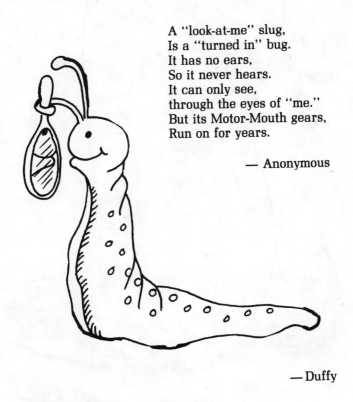

A "look-at-me" slug,
Is a "turned in" bug.
It has no ears,
So it never hears.
It can only see,
through the eyes of "me."
But its Motor-Mouth gears,
Run on for years.

— Anonymous

— Duffy

Slug Trail 8

Basic Standard Slugs

These slugs are so much a part of our lives that we hardly notice them. They slowly accumulate until we feel down but don't know the reason. These slugs are like sandpaper that rubs across your sense of self slowly until you feel sensitive and worn out.

We pick up these slugs everywhere: on the road where another driver makes faces at us because he thinks we made a mistake; or in parking lots or lines where someone doesn't want to wait his turn. BASIC STANDARD slugs are very rude.

You can find a lot of these slugs at stores. People will stare at you because they think you look different or in some way unacceptable to them. Clerks who are in a bad mood will snap at you or treat you with disdain. "I'm looking for a purple dress, please." "My dear, no one is wearing purple this year."

These slugs float around home and work with abandon. They are often disguised as teasing or joshing. "Hey Mary, your hair looks like you put your finger in an electrical socket! Just kidding, old girl." "You look just awful; are you sick or something?" "This is my smart child, and this is my sweet child." "You could really look nice if you tried a little harder."

The hardest thing about these slugs is recognizing them for what they are, power plays. The slug-giver keeps you one down and himself up. The best way to handle these slugs is to counter with a positive act. Let another motorist in ahead of you, compliment the store clerk or co-worker, and smile benignly. They know you know what they are and what they are handing out, and that's enough.

Last night I came home after receiving test results for my first exam in a college anatomy course. I was happy to tell my perfectionist husband that I received a "B." He said very seriously, "Don't worry, honey. I'm sure you'll do better next time."

Wife: "Honey, you really should fix the leaking pipe in the kitchen."

(Later, after Honey has spent two hours under the sink with skinned knuckles and water dripping in his face.)

"How are you doing, honey? Perhaps we should call a plumber before you break something."

My boss handed me a bunch of pennies to get him some coffee. At a distance of 20 feet, I looked them over and said, "Wow, this one is an Indian head!"

He said, "They're valuable, aren't they?"

I said, "They sure are," and put it in my pocket. From that day on he was able to go and buy his own coffee.

"You're so boring that I'll bet when you pray God falls asleep."

Response: "I'm sorry. You'll have to repeat that, I have a hard time concentrating on monotonous voices."

My newly-wed husband and I were having dinner at the home of my mother-in-law. There were about a dozen or so people all sitting around her dining room table when the conversation turned to one of the neighbors, who was dating a girl from the same street I grew up on. My mother-in-law said, "Well, I wouldn't think much of her then, because every person on that street is nothing but a snob!"

With potatoes, rolls, and steak fixed to perfection, the wife announced that dinner was ready. Her husband's retort, "Steaks cost so much. Next time, let me cook them, and they will be hot and just right WHEN WE want them."

Husband will ask his wife's opinion and then, if he doesn't like the response, will say, "Oh well, what do YOU know!"

"I really admire your doing the kind of work you do. My pride would get in the way."

"My, you're looking so much better than the last time I saw you."

A co-worker said, "Pregnancy has swelled your breasts. They've gone from tiny to small."

Susan Dixon

I picked out a greeting card in the department store, found a clerk, gave her the card and some money, and she took them to a cash register out of sight. I waited and waited, and other customers around me were waiting. I decided that she had gone to lunch, or perhaps had resigned, when she came back carrying my card in a little sack. She looked over the crowd. I waved and said, "Here I am." She looked at me and said, "Oh, I thought it was someone younger." I replied, "When you left, I *was* younger."

I told a friend that my house had been appraised at $_____. She said, "Oh boy, if you can get that much for yours, imagine what I can get for mine."

Co-worker about another co-worker: "I don't like her mouth. The lower teeth are set farther in than the upper, and the upper teeth are too large...You know, like your mouth."

I have a neighbor who is very competitive about our children and is always frustrated about the early progress of my one child. On the afternoon that I told her he had begun to crawl, she replied, "Oh, I can't wait until he drinks kerosene or gasoline."

My mother, who has devoted her life to keeping a house in which you can eat off the floors, has found me to be a housekeeping disappointment. I have taken many slugs, such as, "You can't get GOOD vacuuming from an 8-year-old," and "If you didn't have all these plants, animals, kids and activities, you wouldn't have this dust problem."

She spied a cobweb (an old one) in my kitchen corner one day and said, "What is THAT?" I replied, "A science project."

Mom to me: "You've two little, beady pig eyes."

Mom to me: "You should have been a boy. Look at yourself—big hands, big feet, big shoulders. You're BIG all over."

"Who wants to go to the party tonight?"

I said, "I'll go," rather meekly.

Question is repeated and I say again, louder, "I'll go."

Reply: "I know you'll go, but doesn't anyone else want to go?"

From my older sister:

"You're always so afraid to do things. What a dummy! You're cruel and thoughtless."

From my older brother:

"You did good—you didn't burn dinner this time. Did you really make this?"

"When are you going to develop a bustline?"

From my younger sister:

"You've never liked me."

"You're so ugly you must need to wear two bags over your head in case one rips."

"Gee, you look marvelous! Did you have plastic surgery?"

Husband:
"You are the worst 'slop can' I have ever met."
Wife:
"Thank you. I work really hard to stay at the top of your list."

My mom says she'll quit smoking when I get my life together, so if she dies of cancer, I'm to blame.

My boyfriend says to me, "You know what's at the end of a rainbow", a blond with big boobs." I am a blond with a small chest.

My favorite ethereal slugs: "I don't think you'll be able to understand." and "It would be a waste of time explaining it to you."

You never do anything right!

I'm sorry I married you!

You'll never amount to anything!

A new woman was hired at work to serve in a position equal in stature to mine. Upon meeting me, she sat across from my desk and proceeded to "get acquainted." After talking for a few minutes, we discovered that we had attended the same college. She inquired as to what year I had attended. I told her, 1969. With disbelief in her eyes she said, "Wow, you must have waited several years after high school before you started college! 1969 is when I attended!" I went to college right after high school and we found out that we were the exact same age.

Employer Slug:
"If you don't do things my way, you are incompetent."

Upon realizing that I was 15 minutes late for work, I ran out the door and up the street. I heard my bus roll on down the highway. Determined to deal with reality and take charge of the situation, I called my place of work and let them know I'd be late. I patched up my guilt feelings by telling myself, "Hey, Ellen, you're an okay person, whether you are late or not. You come out okay either way. Give yourself credit for taking responsibility for your tardiness."

The next bus pulled up, and I greeted the driver with a warm "Hello" and a smile.

She responded with a time-released slug: "You're late again, huh?"

Husband: "I find it really hard to read when you're making noise gathering up the trash."

Wife: "Why don't YOU gather the trash, and I'll see if I can manage to read."

Old Family Slug

My husband and I were teaming up to capture a mouse when it slipped past him and escaped. I snapped "What the hell's the matter with you, anyway?" I suddenly realized where it came from. I'd heard it countless times growing up. I apologized for the slug as I recalled stories of my Uncle Tom, who was great fun for us kids. Uncle Tom was once playing monster by standing on the toilet with a towel over his head. When the kids all ran out screaming, my grandfather made a trip to the bathroom and exploded, "What's going on here? What the hell's the matter with you, anyway?" All Uncle Tom's antics around my grandfather would be followed by that slug.

So I have vowed, "The slug stops here."

Most obnoxious slug:
Twenty-one year old upstart supervisor talking to an older employee: "Do I have to hold your hand to get anything done?"

Susan Dixon

When I cut my son's hair in years past, my son would say, "Dad, can't you cut my hair so it wouldn't be so short?" I would reply, "I only know how to cut men's hair. If you want long hair, you'll have to get your mom to cut it."

Quote from Giovanni Guardeschi, "My Home, Sweet Home":
    "The man who offers an insult writes it in sand, but for the man who receives it, it's chiseled in bronze."

Slug Trail 9

Terminal Slugs

These slugs are almost beyond belief. They are usually associated with death and the level of their insensitivity boggles the mind. You have just buried your dear beloved wife, and one of her friends mentions to you that the dress you carefully chose to bury her in was one she always hated.

You or a friend are disabled, and someone either imitates you, is overly solicitous, turns away in disgust, or mentions loudly enough for you to hear, "People like that shouldn't be allowed to live," or "Can't they at least stay inside?"

One way to handle terminal slugs is with sympathy for the terrible condition of the psyche and soul of the slug-giver. He must be really sad. Comment that you are: "Sorry that you seem to need to hurt people," or offer to help him with his obvious problem.

With my mother's permission I purchased, at age 12, a bottle of Avon's "Lily of the Valley" cream perfume. After I had it for about a week, I worked up enough courage to wear it to school. I came home for lunch from the 6th grade of a rather strict parochial school and placed some fragrance on each wrist and behind my ears, just like a big lady. I returned to school just in time to run up the stairs and take my seat. As I was sitting and feeling very grown up, smelling wonderful, a girl walked by to hang up her coat and said, it a loud voice, "WHO DIED?"

My mother took a dislike to my son partly because he was reserved and did not display the amount of affection toward his grandmother that she wanted. She said, "You should do something about Richard. You know, Charles Manson was awfully unfriendly when he was a kid, too."

I was seven when my father died very suddenly. I did not really feel that he had died. At the funeral, I heard a woman say to a friend, "Pearl must not have loved her daddy very much. She has not cried at all since his death." This, to me, was the ultimate slug of my life, and I am 53.

With two babies and a husband who worked swing shift, I was not able to go to church three times a week. After my two-year-old son died, the pastor's wife said to me, "God sometimes takes our children when we're not good parents."

"After my second mastectomy within a period of 2 months, my aunt said to me, "Well, at least you're not lopsided."
My doctor's nurse said, "You might as well die from cancer as from anything else."
My mother read the obituaries to me.

My favorite, if that's possible, violent slugs:

I'm doing this for your own good!

Why do you make me hit you?

I wouldn't beat you if I didn't love you.

This hurts me more than it hurts you!

I had been water skiing for a long time, I asked my dad to teach me how to ski on one ski, he turned to me and said, "I bet you $10.00 you'll never make it."

After waiting for the birth of my first child and being fearful because my mother had lost her first child, I began to despair since I was 3½ weeks overdue. One afternoon, the phone rang and it was my aunt. She wanted to know why I was so late in delivering and she further inquired, "Is the doctor sure the baby isn't dead inside of you."

Comment from mother after her daughter has lost a baby with S.I.D.S. and has a second child with cerebral palsy:
"What's your problem that you can't seem to have a normal baby?"

"You're the hardest person in the world to live with."

A retroactive slug, "to be read in the event of my death" from a perfectionist parent:
Dear Child,
I am sorry I have failed so badly as a parent to you. I have failed to make you happy. I have failed to help you have a worthwhile life. Please forgive me; I tried so hard for you.
Love,
Comment: How can I hand this slug back?

The Cremation Slug

A young friend of my husband was killed in a tragic accident. He was seriously disfigured, and his wife chose to have him cremated. At the wake following the funeral, one of her husband's ex-girlfriends came up to her and said, "How could you have him cremated? I didn't get to say good-bye. Now I'll never get over his death."

Young Slugs*

Children have the largest slug collections of all. It takes a lot of growing up or an advanced sense of humor to realize that what adults are saying is not always true. Kids tend to believe adults don't have problems and are telling the truth. Help!

Under the guise of teasing, kidding, competition and constructive criticism we beat up anyone young enough to be taken advantage of.

"Look at the size of her feet!"

"I hope she's smart because her sister is much cuter."

"You look like a barn in that outfit. How did you get so big?"

I remember as a scared new mother when someone glanced at my three month old. "Does he turn over yet?" I didn't know so I said "Maybe." She answered, "Oh, my baby turned over in the birth canal." My son had heard his first slug.

Parents

Parents deliver the biggest ones because they are just repeating a pattern they learned as children, they feel competitive with their kids, or they cannot tell the difference between encouragement and criticism.

Some parents are so afraid that their children will think well of themselves and become conceited that they neither compliment them nor allow them to accept compliments.

"She may look good to you but you should see the way she keeps her room."

"He could do much better if he wanted to."

"We can't imagine that he'll ever amount to anything."

Imagine a four year old who walks into the kitchen and sees a bowl of cherries, her favorite thing. What's the normal impulse? To eat them all, of course! Her mother comes in and sees her stuffing them in.

"Oh Julie, I'm so disappointed in you. I didn't know you were such a selfish little girl." As the child begins to shrink in shame, Mom delivers the next blow. "You are a little pig, a selfish little pig, nobody likes a greedy guts."

There are other ways to teach kids to be unselfish without shaming them forever.

"You sure love cherries, don't you? Well so do I but if you eat them all the rest of the family won't be happy about it. I'm going to put the rest away since you've had your share."

The child gets the same message but without being wrapped in a slug she doesn't know how to handle or defend herself against.

Parents deliver giant prediction slugs as a way of exercising power and putting a child down. They don't realize that the kids will follow their lead. They will believe what the parent said and it can become a self-fulfilling prophecy.

"With a face like that you'll never get married."
"Anyone who sees your room won't want to be your friend."
"You've ruined my life. If I hadn't had you I would have
_____."
"You are always a problem."
"You're on your way to hell in a hand basket."
"I'll never be able to trust you again."
"I suppose you'll never be able to do any better."
"You're a slut."
"I'm very disappointed in you."
"I can't count on you.
"You never do anything right."
"You'll be the death of me yet."
"You're driving me crazy!"

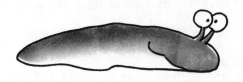

Relatives, teachers, neighbors and even strangers hand slugs to kids in front of adults and no one does anything about it.

"You couldn't hit the ball if your life depended on it."
"He's awfully small for his age."
"Can't you do anything with him."
"Her cousin is a much better child."
"You are invited but don't bring him."
"What happened to her face?"
"You're not the only student I have."
"Don't you ever consider anyone else's feelings?"
"Why aren't you more like your brother?"

Kid To Kid Slugs

Perhaps the toughest situations, especially for teenagers, are the slugs they get from each other. Peers will tease about looks, clothes, intelligence, family, personality, cool, coordination — everything about image. They will bark as you go by to let you know they think you're a dog. They'll suggest you wear a paper bag over your head.

They do it because they are scared. They've been raised on constant comparison and competition and every day they must jockey for position to feel they have any value. Kids who deliver a lot of slugs are kids who have been given a lot of them. It's natural to try and unload some on anyone within striking distance.

Here are some samples of the current slugs in the middle school set. Add your own if you've got a collection.

"Your hair doesn't look bad for a change."
"Hey, zithead!"
"Don't you have any other clothes? You always wear the same thing."
"Wow, you're almost as cute as your dog!"
"Hey, tinsel teeth, how are you?"
"You smell."
"What are all those spots on your face? Been eating with a fork again?

We all recognize big mean slugs like "I don't want you" or "I wish I'd never had you." But even very young children pick up slugs.

One teacher asked first graders what hurt them and this is their list:

"When older kids laugh at me and tease me because I'm little."

"When you're talking and they turn their back on you."

"When they say 'nani, nani' or say 'so!'"

"Sometimes they'll play with everyone but me."

"When they tell jokes or secrets about you."

"Being called 'baby.'"

"I don't like my brother to pick on me."

"They make up names for me that are nasty."

"Sticking tongues out or thumbs down."

"When they roll their eyes to show they don't like you."

Very perceptive for children who are only six or seven.

Third graders were asked about slugs and how to turn them into butterflies. Their answers were wonderful. We might wish adults could be as perceptive.

"When my sister starts following me I sometimes push her but after I've thought about what I did my heart tells me I'd better say sorry."

"I don't like it when kids call me 'bucktooth,' 'beaver,' and 'chipmunk.' But I know when I'm older I can get my teeth straightened."

65

"I hate when people say shut-up to me because it makes me want to say it back."

"Slugs that we turn into butterflies are when someone is about to beat you up. You say nice things to them and then they don't beat you up."

"It's like when you're mad at somebody and you make up."

"When you take something that is 'someone else's and they know and then you tell the truth and you're friends again."

"If you're going to say something mean to someone and you say something nice to them instead."

Slugs follow children all the way through school. These are from some fifth graders.

"When people think you're dumb because you come from a family with problems or when you come from another country."

"When you're doing something that you don't know how to do and your friend says, 'I can do that better than you.'"

"When no one wants you on their team it's a real bad slug."

"When the friends you always play with say you can't play, you always cry a little."

"When people try to to make you do what you don't want to do."

"When I am sick and miss something and people tell me how much fun it was and say I shouldn't have missed it."

"When someone always says something rotten and then says just kidding."

"Someone told me, "If you were any worse at sports you'd have to be in the special olympics."

"You're so black I can't tell you from the chalkboard."

"If you touch me I'll have to be quarantined."

Name Calling

poem

They call me "four eyes," "brace face," "blubber body," too,
Say I'm so ugly that I belong in the zoo.
Being called names makes me feel so bad,
That I wish they'd just stick with the name that I have.

'Cause I can read music and I can do math,
Make soap monsters when I take a bath.
Why should how I look make them all laugh?
It's true that it really, really, really, really hurts when they do.

They call me "knock-kneed," "baby faced,"
    "dummy, dumb, dumb,"
Say that I'm such a wimp that I can't even run.
Why can't they be nicer and just let me be.
'Cause there's lots of good things about people like me!

Anonymous

Adults Can Help

Teachers and parents can hold slug contests so children will hear that everyone gets them. They hurt but we can laugh at them. After a contest there is an immediate jump in the self-esteem of the kids. They hurt less and fewer kids are willing to hand out slugs since they know they can get caught with "Wow, that's a winner, that's a slug of the month, let's turn it in for a prize."

Teenage Sluggers

Teen-age slugs are the toughest category. I cleaned these up since using gross words is part of their style.

"You get such good grades. Do you cheat?"
"I wish I had your feet, then I could ski for free."
"When you were born they slapped your mother."
"Was your nose broken."
"Your socks match your earrings."
"Still riding the bus, huh?"
"If I were you I wouldn't have done that."
"You could have found someone better than him."
"You look a lot like your mom. She's got a weird face."
"Even you should be able to understand that!"

"You only do that to get attention."
"Hey, geek!"

You can add your own favorites and the ones I was afraid to print. Once kids understand what a slug is, give yourself and your friends ways to fight back.

Ways To Fight Back

I mentioned contests and rewards for the best slug but just keeping a record helps. When Dad tells you how awful you look get out a notebook and ask him to repeat it so you can write it down for your collection. Criticism is toxic. Get it out of your head and on to paper. Create your own toxic waste dump.

Keep a positive/negative notebook page for a criticizing teacher or classmate. Every time they make a remark to you put it down as a negative or positive. Make it obvious that you're keeping a score.

Understand that the idea is to put you down and how you handle it determines how you feel. It doesn't help to fight back because the slugs will multiply and do in both of you. Here are some comebacks that work:

"You sure know how to hurt a guy."
"Wait until my psychiatrist hears that one."
"Amazing, but true."
"You're right and it's going to get worse."
"No-o-o! Really?"
"I couldn't agree with you more."
"I just love your sense of humor."
"I've really enjoyed talking with you."
"I'd like to think about this and discuss it with you later."
"Would you put that in writing for my collection."
"That was supposed to be a secret."

Use your sense of humor by making anything and everything into a joke:

Slugger: "You're so ugly you need to wear two bags over your head in case one of them rips."
Response: "It always helps to be prepared."

or

"Ohh, I'm glad you noticed."

Slugger: "You'll eat anything. You are the worst slop can I've ever seen."
Response: "It's great to be number one."

or

"I'm a real pro."

Sometimes it helps, especially with adults to let them know that you know they are out to hurt:

"Thanks for the confidence booster."
"I love getting compliments."
"Well, it's been fun talking to you."
"Ouch!"
"That hurts!"
"Direct hit!"

To survive happy in this world you need three skills: flexibility, a sense of humor, and self-esteem. There are hundreds of ways, using these skills, to see a slug coming and send it into outer space. The important thing is to know that some people have book bags, pockets and purses full of them and they'll hand them to anyone who appears to be a taker. As soon as they know you are on to the "game" they will leave you alone. Nothing hurts a slug giver more than being caught in the act. If your parent or teacher is the slugger be careful and very diplomatic. When you take care of yourself they lose a little power and may shift to other power plays.

Check your attitude and your own slug throwing tendencies so you can save your energy and enjoy your life.

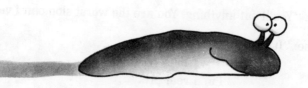

Last Minute Slugs

"When I played basketball and I lost my first game, my dad walked up to me and said, 'Hi loser.'"

"I was walking and I had short pants on and someone asked, 'Where's the flood?'"

"This kid's dad told him he had 'crap for brains' and the kid felt real bad and didn't know what to say."

"I was looking at some clothes and a kid said, 'Your Mom and Dad don't have enough money to buy that sweater.'"

"I was over at a friend's house to spend the night. We were in a fight and she said to me, 'You jerk! I never liked you anyway. I just said I did so I wouldn't hurt your feelings.'"

"My mom said I wasn't wanted and she blamed her having too many children on me."

"A classmate said that I should have been kidnapped. It hurt me because it was so frightening."

"I was talking to one of my friends and I started my sentence 'I think ...' and she said, 'That's a first' and went off laughing."

"Once when I was going to my classroom from the bus some kids started to laugh at me and I couldn't figure out why. They said, 'You're ugly and your clothes don't match!'"

"I was walking by the spider bars and a boy was talking to all the 'cool kids.' All of a sudden he screamed, 'What's bigger than her lips?' I almost cried."

"A kid at school said to me, 'You're a smelly, dirty, no good, skinny weakling!' All I was doing was playing softball."

*Thank you McGilvra School, Issaquah Middle School, and Marysville-Pilchuck High School.

The Need To Be Right

A close cousin of perfectionism is the need to be right. This need leads to a veritable deluge of slugs. Slugs become the weapon of first choice in the great fight to be right. The need to be right is usually the need to feel you are valuable because you doubt your self-worth. Therefore you are always out to prove your worth at the expense of other people.

The time for decision is here. Do you want to be right or happy? You can only be one. Now I know some of you are saying "How can I be happy if I am not right?"

First of all I am not talking about the need to be right on crucial issues such as the stress factors on bridges, the chemical contents of prescriptions or whether you shoot someone or not. Those decisions make up only about two percent of our lives. I am talking about the other 98% where it is not only unimportant to be right but hard to tell who is and who isn't. But, we will still fight over it. Check yourself, what do you need to be right about:

Socks

There are people who fight over the right way to roll socks. They are still nibbling at each other after twenty years of different opinions. There are many ways to roll socks. There are rollers, folders, those who turn down the cuff and those who don't. There are those who tie socks in knots, those who buy fancy socks that snap together and those who throw them in the drawer. There are even two kinds of throwers. Those who throw them in the drawer and spread them around so the drawer will shut and those who just throw them in and force the drawer shut.

Who is right? Well you were taught by someone who told you it was the right way. They were taught the same thing. But there is no right way. There is only your preference which is based on someone else's preference.

A friend of mine ran into a terrible dilemma. She was a roller and her husband a thrower. She had carped for years. Then her mother came to visit — the same mother who had taught her to roll socks, tightly. Her mother was helping to put away the laundry and she was throwing the socks into the drawer in a pile. When questioned she said, "Oh, I changed years ago!"

Loading Dishwashers

Have you carped recently to your family about whether the forks go up or down in the dishwasher? There is no evidence to support either up or down only your preference. If you ask your family to do it right they will do it wrong just to frustrate you. Instead say to them, "I sleep better at night when the forks are up in the dishwasher, it's just a preference I have." They will want to please you and you won't have to hand out any more slugs.

Navigation

This starts some of the worst fights.

You're in a car. You're the passenger. Your husband is driving. "Dear, did you mean to make that left turn?" "Yep, always go this way." "Well, you know that's not the best route." "I think it's the best route. I think it's the right route." "Well, dear, we're going to be late."

Now if you're smart, you'll stop talking right then because there are two right routes, at least. There's the one that he knows that always gets him there and there's the one you want. But, even if you stop talking you may sit there and seethe, "That fool, he thinks he knows the right way."

By the time you get to the party or the meeting, you two may be snarling at each other. What's the right way? There's probably about 25 right routes from here to there. So next time you're in a navigation argument, if you're not driving, keep quiet. The person who's driving gets to choose the right route and you get to choose to be happy.

Children

We often confuse our preferences as adults, which you're entitled to, with the "right" way. Children are confused by this. We say "do it right," and insult them if they don't. Yet, still being open to the world they see lots of good ways to do things.

I had a little boy call me, and he was mowing the lawn. His mother said "do it right." He was mowing the lawn his way, but she wanted the lawn mowed her way. She said, "Do it the right way," and it started a fight. Now he said, "There are lots of ways to mow a lawn. You can mow it diagonally, you can start outside and mow in, you can mow it it chunks. There were lots of ways to mow a lawn." His brain hadn't yet been squeezed into a system that says there's only one right way to do everything.

Now if his mother had said instead, "John, I want you to mow the lawn this way because it's the way my father used to mow it, and it makes me feel secure," he would have been glad to comply. But she said, "Do it right," and that offended his sense of logic. Insist on your preferences if you want to. You don't even have to explain why. But don't insist on being right.

Mistakes

How many mistakes did you make this week? A full life requires thousands of mistakes if you plan to live up to your creative potential.

When we are children, adults try to talk us out of making mistakes and we get confused. They are referring to life-threatening mistakes, but we think they mean everything.

Check how open you are to mistakes. Can you stand it? Can you laugh? Do you shy away from things you might not do well? Do you laugh at people who seem clumsy or naive? Do you grit your teeth when someone you love makes a mistake? Are you under the illusion that everyone is watching you and keeping score?

Start counting your mistakes on a daily basis and try to increase them by 10 percent. That will require you to stretch and grow. Try not mentioning other people's mistakes. Take risks; be tolerant of yourself and others.

Congratulate others on the risks they take; admire their courage. You'll have more pleasure and be much closer to what you want to be. Mistakes are the dues of a good and full life. Stretch and enjoy.

Laws of the Universe

There are many sources of slugs in the world, they don't just come from under the rocks in our psyches. They also lurk around in our perception of the world. Some of us have an erroneous view of the way the world works and it leaves us with an endless supply of slugs.

There are those of you, for example, who believe that you should be able to live in your house with your family and not lose anything. "If they would just be careful and thoughtful you would only need three combs, two pairs of scissors, one Phillips screwdriver, one nail clipper, one hammer, etc."

Then when you cannot find what you need you run screaming around the house calling them names and telling them you cannot stand living with people who never put anything back where they found it.

The Laws of the Universe, in contrast to your view, state very clearly that in the average household over a lifetime you will need:

> 652 combs (add more if you have teenagers),
> 76 pairs of scissors,
> 12 Phillips screwdrivers,
> 82 nail clippers,
> 23 hammers.

Buy cheap ones by the dozen, or on sale. For those of you who are trying to hide one good pair of scissors, please understand that it is impossible. You will have to wait until you are very old and living all alone. Of course, then you will not be able to remember where you put them.

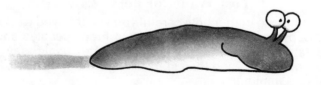

Car Key Law

The Law states very clearly that you need to have five sets of car keys. Yet many of you try to get by with two and suffer the consequences. When your spouse, for example, loses his or her car keys you must immediately scramble and start looking for them until they are found or you could end up in a big fight. You'll get criticized for things that have nothing to do with lost car keys. Buy some extra sets today.

Lost Things Law

There is no way to live up to your full potential in life without losing lots of things. Yet, there are people who believe you can go through a lifetime without losing anything if you would just be more careful and more thoughtful. They actually believe that a child can get through elementary school without losing a jacket. But that's impossible unless the child is repressed. A truly creative child will lose two jackets. Now you can make him contribute to replacing the jacket. It's important to teach responsibility. But don't assume that if they'd just be more thoughtful, that they wouldn't lose anything.

Understand and recognize the laws of the universe and don't get mad. The creative person who lives her life up to its full potential will lose thousands of things. We don't have control over lost things, only in how we perceive a loss and how we handle it.

Dead Battery Law

There are varying quotas on dead batteries. Mine happens to be very high. I assume about 92 in a lifetime so I always carry two sets of jumper cables and get big strong batteries. When I find I have a dead battery I just say "Oh here's number 41." I get a friend or a cab, jump it and am on my way. Once I ate a quick lunch from a roadside vendor while waiting for the cab. I still get dead batteries but no grief.

Lost Wallet or Purse Law

Assume, no matter how careful you are, that you will lose a few. Copy your credit cards, take out irreplaceables and accept fate. When one is lost, allow a brief panic, say "Oh, here's number 3" and then start taking care of the loss. Keep grief to a minimum.

Broken Things Law

There are, of course, those who believe nothing should get broken or spilled. The creative life requires you to spill thousands of things and to break at least 7,683 things or you may be repressed. Check your record.

Check how you respond when other people break things. Do you treat children differently than adults. Children are supposed to break more things. Do you offer a way to replace the item, such as working for it or having it fixed. Or do you grasp the opportunity to unload a few more slugs?

There are many Laws and you can figure out the ones that apply to your life. My favorite of all time, is the: *Toilet Roll Law.*

Toilet Roll Law

There are some of you out there who think that anyone in a household can be taught to put the toilet paper on the toilet roll. That's not true. The law actually says that in any given household only one person will voluntarily put the toilet paper on the toilet roll.

Now if you've got more than one person willing to do it in your house, then that's because they've been carped at, and as soon as they leave home, they'll never put the toilet paper on the roll again.

I found out that I was the designated toilet roll person in my house, and I tried to fight it. I even hired a housekeeper two afternoons a week, and I taught her how to put the toilet paper on the roll, and she nodded.

I left her notes, but in two years she has never once put the toilet paper on the toilet roll. I have, finally, accepted the Law of the Universe, that I'm the designated person, and it has brought me peace of mind.

Classified Section

Whole Slug Catalog
Useful tool and gift ideas

Slug Wrench
For extraction of deep slugs; perfect for salted (retroactive) slugs, swallowed inadvertently. Also called by its advocates "the happy slughooker." $9.95
(Add $3.00 west of the Slugalachians)

Slug Shot
Perfect as medium-range slug projectiles. If the person who is normally your slug recipient has started handing back your slugs, you can get him/her from the back and with a great enough buffer zone so there's no return.

Wood	$4.95
Steel	9.95
Silver	14.95

Slugger
(formerly known as the baseball bat)
If people won't accept your slugs, and you haven't found enough pleasure in seeing your slug recipient being hit in the back with one of your little slimers (even with our slingshot), try our slugger model!
(No ball required.) It provides instant pain!
CAUTION! The major advantage of using slugs for eliciting pain is the freedom from legal and community disapproval. This model slugger does not have those advantages. $14.95

Slugskin

Perfect for making slugs feel comfy until you pass them out for lunches or charming dinners! They'll stay at home until you need them.

$.95 each, $8.00 per dozen

Slug Rope

Braided by primitive ladies in Slugmania; old world charm, absolutely authenic. You can tie yourself up (and everyone in your family) with this marvelous modern invention. $2.95

Slug Rule

An instrument consisting in its simple form of a method of calculating whether the slimy thing in your hand is an AUTHENTIC slug or just an escargot that has been thoughtfully cooked and then removed from its shell.

Services Available

Mainlining Slugs:

The addict seeks out (and always pays for) the best and strongest slugs available. Much of his/her life becomes such a pursuit of this material that other activities become almost impossible. When one source dries up, he/she rushes around to find new slug sources.

Dial-A-Slug:

A special service of the community of slug-donors. The addict can call up any time of day or night and he/she will be issued FREE OF CHARGE-NO OBLIGATION—a slug through the miracle of modern electronic communication.

Book Review

Slug Hug
A manual on how to give a slug. There is a certain way of bestowing affection that will make the hugged person uneasy. This is a talent that anyone can attain through study of this manual. You can make them squirm, and (guaranteed) they will not dare tell you not to do it again.
Profusely illustrated.
                    by Mike Mallace $13.95

Slug Gourmet Cuisine   by Julia Slugchild
Special attention to authentic slug cuisine from all over the world. Slugs are served at fine homes and restaurants worldwide. Among the marvelous recipes: Stir-fried slugs (many textures for the slug eater's palate), After dinner slugs (well-oiled), Slugs a la carte (perfect for picnics), Slugs con carne (the slug-eater's carne, of course), Slug a la creme (you whip them up with enthusiasm and they barely know that under it all is a common slug), etc.

Sing Along With Slug Songbook   by Leopold Slugowski
   All the best songs to slug by: words, sheet music included. "To Know Him Is To Slug Him," "I Can See Clearly Now, The Slugs Have Gone" (included for those who are members of Slugoholics Synonymous or on the slug wagon), "Slug Angel," "Sweet Slugteen," "Slugging Safari."
                 Pop Catalog $7.98

Slugoven's 9th; Slugphony Pathetique; Pictures at a Slugposition; The Barber of Slugville; highlights from Wagner's *Flying Slugman, Slugfried, Gotterslugamerung;* etc.
                 Classical Catalog $7.98

"Put Your Lips a Little Closer to the Slug," "They Can't Take the Slug Out of This Cowboy's .22," "One-Night Slimeance," "Low Rent Slugeroo," "Let Me Go, Slugger."
                 Country-Western $7.98

Manual On Slugging For Success:
Traditional Slug Attire For The Office
   For the rising young doctor, executive, or junior executive. There are many refinements discussed for your climb up the "ladder." You can translate those fine slug-donor instincts you perfected in pre-med chemistry (altering other students' lab experiments) into Brooks Brotherslugs. There are also chapters on advice for the corporate spouse and his/her slugs, training your children to learn to give slugs and not get them, etc. An invaluable aid.
              by Richard Nixslug Associates $29.95
              Available only in hardback

Manual On Transcendental Slugitation

For those who are not content to live in the crude capitalist-run system that surrounds us, where crude, non-spiritual slugs abound, there is a Higher Spiritual Way. (Any semblence to our 1980 manual, *How You Can Attain Complete Passive Aggresion In Only 36 Steps* is strictly coincidental.) There are chapters on the subtle, spiritual slug: How to arrange someone's travels in the land of the spiritually crazy (by methods such as refusal to converse, refusal to keep your body clean and healthy, etc.). There are chapters on silent slugging: How to slug someone with a mere glance, sigh, gesture, so that no one else will recognize it as a slug! (We have perfected these techniques at our 7th Chakra Institutes in Boulder, Colorado; at Sante Fe; and at the Mendicino Coast.)

by Guru/Gos Slugneesh $9.95

Epilogue

I don't know whether this is the beginning or the end of the Great Slug Contest, but we've enjoyed the laughter and your slugs.

The CSC offers an open mailbox to anyone who has a slug contribution. Someday there may be a second collection, but if not, we are an available burial ground. Send your slug away to a decent burial, complete with appropriate giggles and nyah-nyahs. We will send appropriate badges in recognition of your decision to reduce the world population of slugs by not passing yours on or handing it back. Three cheers for zero population growth.

Slug burials can be arranged by writing to the Community Service Committee and sending a one dollar donation for our good work. We share our profit when there is some, with the Committee for Children. We share our love with all of you.

Jennifer James

Community Service Committee
3903 East James
Seattle, Washington 98122

OTHER BOOKS AND TAPES BY JENNIFER JAMES, PH.D.

Books:

WINDOWS. A word, a moment, a new perspective can change a lifetime. Here are some new windows through which to see your world.

This is the second collection of Jennifer James' commentaries. She offers you a chance for more grace and wit, more humor and quality. The possibility of new choices. There is also within these covers her Nepal journey to the "top of the world." $6.95

SUCCESS IS THE QUALITY OF YOUR JOURNEY. This book is a selection of Jennifer's commentaries. There are over 100 witty, thoughtful and sometimes moving selections that will add optimism and depth to your life. $6.95

LIFE IS A GAME OF CHOICE. This book is made up of twenty-six pages of information with illustrations on how you can find out what you want and make changes in your life. $2.95

Tapes Available:

- **DIRECTIONS FOR CHANGE: EXCELLENCE AND OPTIMISM**
- **SELF-ESTEEM**
- **MANAGING STRESS**
- **PARENTING SKILLS**
- **FAMILY SELF-ESTEEM**
- **SUCCESS IN RELATIONSHIPS**
- **PERFECTIONISM AND SELF-WORTH**
- **ZEST FOR LIFE** (Two tapes: $15.00)
- **CRITICISM**
- **WHEN YOUR PARENTS GROW OLD**
- **BEING SINGLE: CHANGE AND RISK**
- **PEAR PERFORMANCE**
- **HAVING IT ALL**

Tapes – $9.95 each

Special discounts are available for counselors, teachers and non-profit organizations.

All prices include shipping and handling. Send check or money order to: Bronwen Press, 3903 E. James, Seattle, WA 98122.

Adult

Children

© **Inner Cosmos**™
presents
**"Nudges" are Change Agents
When you find it hard to
change, carry one.**

Patterns are hard to break without gentle reminders. Tuck these in your pocket or wallet. Use them as book mark, put them in cards or presents. Pin them up or tape to your dashboard. Give them to people you care about.

ADULT SETS include large map and 30 **catalysts,** retail $4.95
CHILDREN'S SETS include map and 11 **catalysts,** retail $1.95

★ALL IN A WONDERFUL BOX WITH INSTRUCTIONS

ORDER FORM

Name _____

Address _____

_____

Adult sets _____

Children's sets _____

Amount enclosed _____

Send checks to © **Inner Cosmos**™ **3903 E. James, Seattle, WA 98122**